SUNDAY MORNING LIVE

VOLUME 3

Willow Creek Resources™ is a publishing partnership between Zondervan Publishing House and the Willow Creek Association. Willow Creek Resources™ includes drama sketches, small group curricula, training material, videos, and many other specialized ministry resources.

Willow Creek Association is an international network of churches ministering to the unchurched. Founded in 1992, the Willow Creek Association serves churches through conferences, seminars, regional roundtables, consulting, and ministry resource materials. The mission of the Association is to assist churches in reestablishing the priority and practice of reaching lost people for Christ through church ministries targeted to seekers.

For conference and seminar information please write to:

Willow Creek Association
P.O. Box 3188
Barrington, Illinois 60011-3188

SUNDAY MORNING LIVE

VOLUME 3

A Collection of Drama Sketches
from Willow Creek Community Church

Edited by Steve Pederson

ZondervanPublishingHouse
Grand Rapids, Michigan

A Division of HarperCollins*Publishers*

Sunday Morning Live: Volume 3

Requests for information should be addressed to:
Zondervan Publishing House
Grand Rapids, Michigan 49530

Library of Congress Cataloging-in-Publication Data

Sunday morning live.
    1. Christian drama, American. I. Pederson, Steve.
II. Willow Creek Community Church (South Barrington, Ill.)
PS627.R4S8   1993   812'.54080382   92-26029
ISBN 0-310-59221-6 (v. 1)
ISBN 0-310-61361-2 (v. 2)
ISBN 0-310-61441-4 (v. 3)

Edited by Lori J. Walburg
Cover design by Cheryl Van Andel

Printed in the United States of America

97 98 / ❖ CH / 10 9 8 7 6 5 4

*To Steve Sherbondy, Paul Lagerquist, Deb Poling,
and Kathy Pederson—our husbands and wives.*

*If our scripts are basically lines actors read,
your love and support are like the paper under and
around the words. A script contains more paper
than ink—it's easy to miss what supports
and gives form to what we enjoy.
People who read this book will undoubtedly notice
only the words, and not appreciate the paper.
We who wrote it know better.*

Contents

About the Contributors

Donna Hinkle Lagerquist has been a part of the Willow Creek drama team for eleven years and a writer for five. Her sketch *Stolen Jesus* is being adapted into a Canadian Television Christmas special. She and her husband, Paul, and their new infant daughter live in Cary, Illinois.

Judson Poling was drama director at Willow Creek for five years. He continues to serve on Willow Creek's staff in the area of small group leadership training. Judson is also co-author of the *Walking With God Series,* Willow Creek's small group curriculum. Judson holds a Master of Divinity degree from Trinity Evangelical Divinity School. He lives with his wife, Debra, and their two children in Algonquin, Illinois.

Sharon Sherbondy has been a member of the drama team for fourteen years and a writer for eight. Her drama ministry has taken her throughout the United States and abroad. She is a co-author of *Super Sketches for Youth Groups,* a finalist for the Gold Medallion Book Award. She home schools her two children and lives with her husband, Steve, in Elgin, Illinois.

Introduction

In 1975, Willow Creek Community Church began in a rented movie theater in suburban Chicago. Founded with the expressed purpose of reaching the nonchurched, today Willow Creek attracts upwards of 15,000 people to its weekend "seeker services."

Since the beginning, drama has been an integral part of Willow Creek's outreach. Different from traditional church drama, these sketches are short, six- to eight-minute, contemporary vignettes, rooted in real-life experience. Today many churches all over the country, both large and small, are using these sketches as a powerful part of their ministry.

The Message "Set Up"

These sketches are not intended to stand on their own. Rather, they are used to create interest in an issue by grabbing the attention of the audience and getting them to identify with the characters. Also, the sketches do not provide easy answers, but instead raise questions, which the pastor then seeks to answer in the message. Much of the material in this volume may seem "secular," in that there is no specific "Christian" content in the sketch itself. However, when the sketch is performed in connection with a biblically based message that addresses the same question or problem, it takes on spiritual significance. *Keeping Tabs*, for example, presents a character who is possessed by the idea of paying back people for kindness shown toward her. While the theme is comically explored, the point it makes is a serious one. Many have a difficult time accepting the mystery of grace—a gift given with "no strings attached." This "secular" sketch has a strong Christian application when presented along with a message on grace.

This separation of drama and message is a major difference between Willow Creek's approach to drama and that traditionally taken by many churches. While difficult for some people to accept, such a separation is supported by dramatic tradition throughout history. Dorothy Sayers, Christian playwright and novelist, summed it up well: "Playwrights are not evangelists." A dictum frequently repeated to aspiring playwrights is "if you have a message, send it to Western Union." At Willow Creek we try not to abuse drama as an art form by manipulating it to preach a message. Simply put, the sketches clarify the "bad news" so the pastor can bring the "good news."

The Audience "Set Up"

A sketch cannot "set up" a message if viewers do not, in some way, see themselves mirrored in the action. Drama works because people experience vicariously what characters act out on stage. We want to engage not only the minds, but also the emotions of our audience. And drama, which results in high identification, appeals to people's hearts as well as their heads.

At Willow Creek we use contemporary "slice of life" drama, rather than enacted biblical stories, because people more readily identify with characters who act and talk like they do and who confront the same daily issues. This approach helps us earn the right to be heard, because our seekers realize that the church is in touch with the real world, where real people live, work, and struggle. Whether it is the man in *Up on the Roof* who is caught in life's competing and exhausting demands, or the woman in *Driven* who is being crushed by her husband's anger, a character has power to communicate when it is rooted in what the audience can identify with.

We've discovered that the degree of audience identification directly parallels what we call the "reality factor." Drama earns credibility with an audience when it is honest and truthful in how it handles material. If drama comes off simplistic and naïve, or presents clichéd, easy answers, it will not produce the desired result. The gulf between the couple in *Driven* can't be bridged with some simple formula. The final image in *One Step Up, One Step Down* of a man who has essentially wasted his life has power precisely because it is so stark. As the man sits alone, clutching a symbol of his ambition, it is clear he has not discovered what gives life real meaning.

If drama for seekers is to be effective in the church, we must be passionately committed to being real, warts and all. We must avoid easy answers, because they ultimately don't help, even if they sound good. Seekers and believers alike want truth, not a sugar-coated, sanitized version of reality.

In his book *Open Windows,* in a chapter entitled "Pitfalls of Christian Writing," Philip Yancey laments:

> Sometimes when I read Christian books, especially in the fields of fiction and biography, I have a suspicion that characters have been strangely lobotomized. . . . Just as a lobotomy flattens out emotional peaks and valleys, Christian writers can tend to safely reduce life's tensions and strains to a more acceptable level. . . . A perverse fear of overstatement keeps us confined to that flatland realm of "safe" emotions and tensions—a fear that seems incredible in light of the biblical model.

The cause of Christ would be well served if the church would listen to Yancey. For it is truth-telling (which isn't very safe) that not only gives ministry integrity, but also opens up seekers to the possibility of transformation through the power of the Gospel.

Getting Started

The sketch format is a fairly easy way for any church, regardless of size, to begin using drama. A little time, a few simple props, a couple of actors (in some cases just one), and a director are all the necessary elements.

Because sketches are short, the time demand for rehearsals is not excessive. Typically, we spend about four to five hours rehearsing each one. If you are working with relatively inexperienced people, however, it would probably be wise to plan more time. Our four hours is divided into two rehearsals. The actors pick up their scripts one week before the performance. Our first rehearsal is early in the week, during which time we discuss the characters and work out the basic movement (blocking). Because we have only two rehearsals, we ask the actors to memorize the script prior to this rehearsal, with the goal of being off the script by the end of the two-hour session.

For the second rehearsal—in our case, before it is performed for the first service—we rehearse one and a half hours, working on stage with the hand props and furniture we'll be using. During this time we polish the movement, work on character consistency, pacing, and the rise and fall of the action. If movement doesn't look natural because an actor is having a hard time making it look motivated, we change it. After we're off the stage, we run lines or work problem areas of blocking for an additional half to full hour. We also try to relax and enjoy each other's company before the service begins.

For props, we use only that which is absolutely necessary. In other words, we don't use furniture to establish setting, but only if it fulfills a necessary function in the sketch. If, for example, a phone is needed, we would use an end table to set it on. But if nothing needs to sit on the end table, why use one? Typically we do not use door or window units. If a window is called for, we mime it. However, rather than mime the opening and closing of an imaginary door, which gets cumbersome, the actors simply enter a room, a convention which an audience seems to accept.

A simple rule of thumb, then, for props and scenic pieces is to keep them simple and rely on the audience's imagination to fill in the details. Not only is this an easier route, but—unless you have a professional set designer—it is also the most effective. Furthermore, since props usually need to be set in place before a sketch and removed afterwards, the simpler you can keep it, the better.

While the technical elements necessary to produce a good

sketch are fairly basic, assembling the right actors and someone to "lead the charge" might prove more challenging. Talent in drama, unlike the other arts, is somewhat difficult to assess quickly. If someone cannot sing a song or play an instrument, it is readily evident, but acting talent is more difficult to define. To further complicate the matter, drama seems to attract people who have an affinity for the arts but who lack specific talent or training. Someone reasons, "I can't sing, or play the piano, but I think I can act." Indeed, maybe this person has acting ability, but too often such people are drawn to drama because it appears relatively "easy," at least compared to the other arts. But doing drama well is more difficult than it appears. Unfortunately, many well-intentioned people, because they know little about the craft of drama, have not helped further the cause of drama in the church. God is not served when drama is done poorly.

Therefore, before getting serious about drama, even short sketches, the church must find a competent drama director. This person needs to have adequate people skills, the ability to assess acting talent, and an understanding of the basics of stage direction. If someone possesses great drama instincts but lacks formal training, it would be a wise investment for a church to enroll this person in some courses in acting and directing at a local college. A good course in directing can provide many of the basic principles necessary for staging drama effectively.

Having formally trained actors is an advantage, but most churches do not have this luxury—all the more reason to have someone with skill and training leading the team. Over time, talented lay people with good dramatic instincts can develop into strong performers, even if they have no previous drama experience, but their growth will be severely limited if their directors do not have sufficient training.

And finally, a word of encouragement. Once a person has understood some basic principles of theatre—as simple as this sounds—that person learns to do drama by *doing* drama. Even the most inexperienced actors and directors can improve, as long as they are willing to learn from their mistakes.

Throughout our many years of doing drama at Willow Creek, we have made numerous mistakes. We still do. In the earlier years, for example, too many of our scripts were "preachy," and therefore stilted and manipulated. Today, periodically, we do a script that we think will work, but it ends up falling flat, due to a lack of conflict, identification, humor, or any number of factors. Sometimes it is particularly frustrating because it's difficult to figure out exactly why a script appeared not to "go over." Such is the business of doing original drama. But as long as we try to learn from each experience, over time we improve the quality and increase our understanding of the craft of drama.

It is our hope that the "tested" resources in *Sunday Morning Live Volume 3,* and others in volumes 1 and 2, will provide you with at least one of the necessary elements for doing drama—the script.

Based on our experience at Willow Creek, these sketches have worked well. We pray they will work well for you, too.

Steve Pederson
Drama Director
Willow Creek
    Community Church

Up on the Roof

Wally, a busy executive, and Vivian, a bag lady, meet in the strangest of places: the roof of an office building. He's there because his boss sent him up to check on their TV reception. She's there to get away from it all. Through their lighthearted conversation and Vivian's homespun wisdom, Wally faces the fact that his life has become overwhelming and he is exhausted. The brief refreshment of the peaceful rooftop gives way to a call from the boss. Wally must return to work, but he has been changed by this most unlikely of teachers.

SUGGESTED TOPICS: emotional refueling, pace of life, learning to be compassionate

CHARACTERS:

Wally   an overworked businessman
Vivian   an affable bag lady with some uncommon insight into human nature

PROPS: old recliner, TV antenna filled with Vivian's "stuff," portable phone, small ladder or step stool

Up on the Roof

Donna Hinkle Lagerquist

Setting: *A man in a suit, harried, walks out on the roof of his office building holding a cordless phone. There is a TV antenna at one end loaded with recognizable debris: a scarf, other articles of clothing, a shopping bag, a dish towel, a hat, an umbrella.*

Wally: *(looking at antenna, amazed)* What in the world? *(dials phone)* Lois? It's Wally. Put me through to Altman. No, I'm not in my office, I'm on the roof. Never mind, Lois, put me through . . . Yeah, Mr. Altman? Wally. I found the "problem" with your TV reception. There's all sorts of debris caught in the antenna. Yes, sir. I'll take care of it. Oh, they're in the top of the second—well, I'll hurry, sir. I know how important those Cub games are, sir. Yes, sir. Will do. Goodbye, sir. *(smiles, hangs up, angry)* I can't believe he sends me up here to do this! *(He sees an old beat-up recliner a few feet away from the antenna.)* How on earth did that get up here? I won't ask. *(He moves chair over to antenna, steps on it to reach debris.)* As if I'm not already swamped. *(starts removing debris)* He wanted the Donaldson quote by 5:00 and McPherson's deficit accounted for . . . and what's he doing? Watching the Cubs! *(Bag lady appears.)*

Vivian: Hey, I bet your momma woulda walloped you for walking on her furniture like that!

Wally: *(shocked, jumps down, hurts back)* Ah! Who are you? Where'd you come from?

Vivian: Just enjoying the view from behind that vent.

Wally: This is *private* property.

Vivian: I know! That's why I like it up here . . . it's real private. I come up here every now and then just to "get away from it all."

Wally: You're living up here?

Vivian: No, just visiting, like a mountaintop retreat. It can be a real rat race down there where I live—I mean, real rats racing! *(laughs, Wally doesn't)* You know, Wally, you should come up here more often . . . get away from all that stress!

Wally: Why would I want to come up to a dirty, unairconditioned rooftop in the middle of the city! And how'd you know my name? Look,

I'm calling the cops *(starts to use phone).*

Vivian: Okay! Okay! I'm leaving . . . Let me see if my things are dry. *(Opens up little step ladder near antenna and climbs up to "debris.")*

Wally: That's your junk on Mr. Altman's antenna?

Vivian: Careful what you call junk, Wally. This here stuff can be treasure. See this scarf? Tells me which way the wind's blowing so I know if a storm's on its way, and see this . . .

Wally: *(interrupts, irritated)* Look! I don't have time to hear about all your . . . "treasure." Just get it off the antenna! And get out of here.

Vivian: Too bad . . . I sure do hate to lose this view of the lake. It's *so* relaxing to watch the boats sail by.

Wally: Yeah, what . . . lake? You can't see the lake from this building!

Vivian: Sure you can! *(Starts pushing chair back to original position.)* Let me put the

chair back where I origi-
nally had it. Takes a little bit
a work, but you get a real
nice view. You sit in it *(does
so)*, recline to about here,
and look off to the right
about two inches, and
there it is, between them
two gray buildings! When
a boat is on that very
piece of the lake, it fills up
the space between the
two buildings! It's so relaxing to watch for them
boats . . . and a lot more
fun than all your problems,
Wally.

Wally: I don't have any problems;
you've got the problem.
Now, here take your . . .
*(Steps on ladder, reaches
up to antenna to get more
of Vivian's "stuff." Strains
back again.)* Ah! *(steps
down)*

Vivian: What's the matter?

Wally: My back—a muscle
spasm. Oh, I hate it when
this happens.

Vivian: Happens a lot, does it?

Wally: *(directed to her)* Only
when I get very tense! Ah!
(screams in pain)

Vivian: Here *(getting up)*. Have a
seat. It'll take the pressure
off. *(She forces him into
the chair. He protests, but
she persists. She removes
his coat in the process;
hangs it on the antenna.)*
Yep, that's a perfect rem-
edy for what's happening
to you!

Wally: *(not so sure)* Yeah!

Vivian: *(trying to lighten him up)* A
full-blown *Mutiny on the
Body*, that's what you've
got. *(laughs)* Ha! *(Wally
doesn't react.)* Wally, you
must be in real bad shape.
Everybody laughs at my
Mutiny on the Body line.

Wally: Yeah? Well, I'm not everybody . . . and it wasn't
funny . . . and quit calling
me Wally!

Vivian: That's your name, ain't it?

Wally: Yes, but . . . but . . . don't
act like you know me . . .
cuz you don't. *(tries to get
up, can't)* Ah! *(Sits back,
long pause as Vivian
crosses back to antenna
and continues removing
items.)* This is really strange.

Vivian: *(thinking he's referring to the chair)* Yeah, you gotta admit, it beats that cast iron stuff they put in the parks!

Wally: *(to himself mostly)* It reminds me of when I was a kid. We'd tell Mom we were going up to get our tennis balls out of the gutter, but we really just wanted to go up on the roof. We would "escape" from everything . . . and what did we have to "escape" back then?

Vivian: Seems to me you'd have the same things back then as you do now . . . as *I* do now . . . too much noise, people pushing you around, telling you what to do, people needing something you got, or just plain needing you too much!

Wally: Boy, don't I know that. *(realizes he's gotten too revealing)* But why am I talking to you like this?

Vivian: *(pulling ladder/stool over to the chair and sitting on it)* Probably because I'm listening. *(Their eyes meet for a moment.)*

Wally: Yeah, life in the fast lane. Nobody listens anymore.

Vivian: Why don't you pull off on the shoulder for a while and change a tire?

Wally: Change? I just changed neighborhoods—bought a house! It's okay, but with a house comes new problems, new responsibilities. Lawn to mow, roof to repair. And the kids, don't get me wrong. I love 'em, but man, they are *work!* The older they get, the more activities they get involved in, thus, the more activities I get involved in!

Vivian: Wally, kids are like a lawn, leave them unattended and they start growing weeds. Before you know it, they're wild. *(reaching in her coat)* Hey, Wally, want a day old bagel?

Wally: *(He's fully reclined, like in a psychologist's office.)* That's another pressure— eating right!

Vivian: No, they soften up real well if you let them set in your mouth for a while.

Wally: *(almost oblivious to Vivian)* My wife keeps setting these articles on cholesterol and heart disease next to my bowl of oat bran and wheat germ with soy milk! Sometimes she cuts out obituaries of 40–50 year old men and sets them on the table with a note saying "You could be next." Now I can't even enjoy a good hot dog with the works without feeling guilty. Eating has become work!

Vivian: You sure don't need more work!

Wally: No! That's just the tip of the iceberg. My "in box" is so full I've had to use my "out box" for my "in box" in addition to my "in box" . . . and things have mistakenly gone "out" before they ever get "in," and then they come back "in" and Mr. Altman wonders why they never got out! You know what I'm saying.

Vivian: Reminds me of when I got stuck in one of them revolving doors at the Marshall Field's. I must of gone around and around for an hour!

Wally: *(not hearing)* I have more deadlines to meet each week than there are days of the week! Deadlines, quotas, more deadlines . . . and he sends me up here to fix his TV reception! I can't keep up!

Vivian: Maybe that's why they're called *dead*-lines!

Wally: *Dead*-lines. Ha! You're right. You kill yourself to meet them! *(They share a laugh, then the phone rings. He starts to get up, but Vivian stops him.)*

Vivian: I'll get it. *(Crosses to his suit coat and removes phone from his pocket.)* Here, I think it's for you!

Wally: Hello? *(gets tense again)* Yes, Mr. Altman. I'm almost finished. No, sir . . . not dawdling. I . . . oh, I ran into a little problem, minor *(to Vivian)*. I'll be right down, sir. Good-bye. *(getting up)* Oh, man! I have two big clients waiting and tons of work, and I'm up here talking to some bag lady!

Vivian: *(She has gotten his suit-coat and is holding it so as to help him on with it.)* Good choice! *(Their eyes meet again, pause.)*

Wally: Yeah, right. *(She helps him with the coat.)* Look, I gotta go . . . next time lay your "stuff" out on the vents over there, will you—not on Altman's antenna! Okay? *(Starts to leave.)*

Vivian: Yeah. Hey, Wally, how's your back?

Wally: Huh? Oh, it's . . . it's pretty good. *(pause, warmly)* Thanks. *(He turns to go once again.)*

Vivian: Ah, Wal, can I tell you something? *(He turns back.)* You know, I handle life one little battle at a time . . . and when one's done I go to the next. I think you got a full scale war that crept up on you . . . a real "mutiny on the body," and now you're surrounded. You gotta take care of yourself, Wally. My chair will be here. You come on up whenever you want, okay? *(Wally nods.)* I'll get my treasures down . . . that'll help you out . . . a little.

Wally: Thanks. Ah . . . *(doesn't know her name)*

Vivian: . . . Vivian.

Wally: Thanks, Vivian. Thanks . . . for listening.

Vivian: Remember, just one little battle at a time. *(He smiles, turns, and leaves as the lights fade on a contented Vivian.)*

Life Cycle

Linda and Ann, strangers next to each other on exercise bikes, discover they have something in common. Both are worn-out moms looking for any excuse to get out of the house. Almost by accident, Linda tells Ann she's in a Bible study group. Although she is self-conscious as she talks more about her faith, an affinity grows between the women. Ann must leave, but after she's gone, Linda "pedals faster" as she realizes the significance of her stumbling but sincere attempt to have a spiritually meaningful conversation with a non-Christian.

SUGGESTED TOPICS: witnessing, making a difference, beginning new friendships

CHARACTERS:

Linda	a likable mom with kids at home but inexperienced at talking with non-Christians about spiritual questions
Ann	also a likable mom; inexperienced at talking to Christians

PROPS: Two exercise bikes

Life Cycle

Sharon Sherbondy

Setting: *Fitness center. Two stationary bikes. Scene begins with Ann riding one of the bikes. She's riding steadily, looking straight ahead, deadpan face. Several seconds later Linda enters with a few grunts and groans and wearily gets on second bike. She rides at a slower pace than Ann. Several moments pass.*

Linda: Oh, will you look at that.

Ann: *(gasp)* Oh, that's disgusting.

Linda: I can't even look.

Ann: Can you believe they let people like that in?

Linda: No. There ought to be a law.

Ann: What do you think she weighs?

Linda: About as much as my right thigh. *(they laugh)*

Ann: So how long have you been coming?

Linda: Since January.

Ann: New Year's resolution?

Linda: Yeah. From 1988. I finally made it in. You?

Ann: For about a year.

Linda: Really?

Ann: Yeah. Well, you know, I'm mostly interested in just toning.

Linda: Right. Me too.

Ann: And getting out of the house.

Linda: Oh, you have kids?

Ann: Oh, yeah!

Linda: How many?

Ann: Too many. How about you?

Linda: Two.

Ann: I'm at their beck and call 24 hours a day—except when I'm here.

(The next series of lines moves quickly.)

Linda: I try having a friend over now and then, but you know how that is.

Ann: I haven't completed a sentence with another adult in my house in years.

Linda: I can't remember the last time I did something exciting.

Ann: Outside of yelling at my kids, this is it for me.

Linda: Who'd have thought life could be so much fun?

Ann: How did this happen anyway? *(pause)* Well, I know how it happened, but the routine, I mean.

Linda: I didn't realize how easy you get into a rut. Every day is the same old thing.

Ann: I leave here . . .

Linda: Stop at Dunkin' Donuts . . .

Ann: Yeah, you work up an appetite at a place like this.

Linda: Sure.

Ann: I go home, watch *Oprah*. Did you see her yesterday?

Linda: No, uh uh. I wasn't home yesterday.

Ann: Here working out, huh?

Linda: Yeah, me and little what's-her-body. No, I was at a Bible study.

Ann: Bible study?

Linda: Every Wednesday. Yep, every Wednesday, for the last two years now six of us have gotten together.

Ann: Is this at your church?

Linda: No. Well, we're all from the same church. We take turns meeting at each other's house. Speaking of which, I've got to go home and clean mine.

Ann: I can have the house spotless and then *they* show up. All my kids have to do is just enter a room and it's like a poltergeist has struck. Toys begin flying all over the place! Drives me crazy!

Linda: I'm picking up all day long. That's all we do. Our lives are a series of pick-ups.

Ann: *(pause)* What do you talk about at your meetings?

Linda: My meetings?

Ann: Yeah, your . . . Bible study.

Linda: Oh. Well, we're all moms so we're trying to figure out how to raise our kids and keep our sanity. In fact, the first thing we all did was memorize the most important Bible verse on child-rearing.

Ann: Oh really? What's that?

Linda: "Thou shalt not kill." *(they laugh)*

Ann: *(pause)* I haven't been to church since I was a kid.

Linda: Boy, not me. I've been going since I was a kid. *(dawns on her that she's talking with a non-churched person, becomes a bit nervous)* You don't go to church?

Ann: Uh uh.

Linda: Oh. *(From this point on, her pedaling gradually increases in speed.)* Well, have you ever thought about going?

Ann: To church?

Linda: Yeah.

Ann: No, not really.

Linda: *(cautious, nervous)* Oh. Well, um, do you know much about, uh, you know, Christianity?

Ann: Not really.

Linda: Not really. *(pedals faster)* Well, if you ever have any questions, I'd be happy to answer them for you.

Ann: I'll keep that in mind.

Linda: *(terror in her face, pedaling even faster)* Do you have any now?

Ann: Questions?

Linda: Yes.

Ann: No.

Linda: Good! *(pedaling goes back to normal)* I mean, you might want to think about it and then, if you wanted, we could talk about it while we're . . . toning.

Ann: Oh, okay. Anything to make the time pass quickly.

Linda: Right. *(awkward pause)*

Ann: You know, I'd like some new ideas on how to handle my kids. What else have you learned?

Linda: Oh, lots. I mean, I was just kidding before when I mentioned "Thou shalt not kill."

Ann: So it *is* okay to kill your kids?

Linda: (laughs) Only in self-defense. *(Buzzer goes off on Ann's bike.)*

Ann: Thank goodness. My legs are dead. *(getting off bike)* Well, maybe I'll see you next week.

Linda: OK. Oh, by the way, my name is Linda.

Ann: I'm Ann.

Linda: Great. Next week then.

Ann: Right . . . Maybe we can talk some more.

Linda: Right. *(pause as Ann leaves)* Wow. I can't believe what just happened. She actually wants to talk more. I guess I didn't mess up too badly. Oh, thank you, Lord. Thank you. And I'll see her next week . . . and we'll talk and . . . who knows, we might even lose weight in the process. This is too good to be true. *(pedaling like a crazy woman)* I love working out!

Blackout

Confessions of an Ad-aholic

Al and Alice are "ad-aholics," individuals addicted to advertisements. They somberly explain how the addiction started, progressed, and eventually ruined their lives. This comedy shows how chasing the American dream of having more can be a nightmare.

SUGGESTED TOPICS: American dream, possessions, material contentment, self-control

CHARACTERS:

Al	a normal American male, but sobered by the grip of ad-aholism in his life (in a comic sort of way)
Alice	female version of the same

PROPS: old overstuffed chair, new overstuffed chair, newspaper, grocery bag, apricot danish

Confessions of an Ad-aholic

Judson Poling

Setting: *A man and a woman standing center stage. Stage right is an old stuffed chair, stage left is a new one.*

Al: *(to audience, serious, almost in a daze)* Hello. I'm Al.

Alice: I'm Alice.

Both: We're ad-aholics.

Al: It's not easy coming out and admitting our addiction to advertisements like this.

Alice: Most people hide their disease behind denial . . . but sooner or later it catches up with you.

Al: We didn't start out this way. No one ever plans to be an ad-aholic.

Alice: But once you take that first look at a sale flyer or ad supplement, well, for the ad-aholic, it's only a matter of time.

Al: I remember after we first got married, it seemed like we were the two happiest kids in the world.

Alice: That's the problem with ad-aholism . . . it strikes even the most innocent of victims.

(The two create a past episode in their life. Alice crosses stage right and sits on the old chair. Al picks up grocery bag from behind the chair and crosses to Alice.)

Al: Hi, hon. Loverboy is back from the store.

Alice: Oh, my knight in shining bell bottoms has returned from his quest! What wonderful booty have you brought back from storming the Piggly-Wiggly?

Al: Well, I realize we're kinda short on cash, but after all, today is our first month anniversary. I thought I'd splurge and get us . . . *(pulls bakery box out of the bag)* apricot danishes!

Alice: Groovy!

Al: Speaking of groovy, wait till you see this.

Alice: What?

Al: *(shows her newspaper)* Look at this ad: isn't that the sexiest car you've ever seen?

Alice: *(looks at paper)* A Plymouth Duster!

Al: Alice, look at that car and then look at ours. How can we start our marriage driving a piece of junk?

Alice: Well, how would we ever be able to afford $2695 for a new car?

Al: I've been thinking that I could work a second shift at my uncle's hula hoop factory. After a couple years I'd pay off the loan.

Alice: Hmmm. A new car would be nice. Maybe I could go back to work too . . . a go-go dancer on weekends! *(looks at paper)* And, maybe with the extra money, we'd also have enough to buy one of these lava lamps. We need some new decor in here.

(They break, go back to "confession scene.")

Al: It wasn't long before the Sunday paper ads weren't enough. I started sneaking peeks at the automotive section in the Sears catalog—and that led to subscriptions . . . True Value, Ace—all the *hard-* ware stuff, delivered in plain brown wrappers. I told my wife I liked the articles.

Alice: It was hard for me to keep down a job. I'd stay in bed all day with a splitting headache from a service

Al: merchandise binge the night before.

Al: It got so that we wouldn't even go into a restaurant without taking at least three copies of the real estate ad paper from the foyer.

Alice: When the kids came along, I turned to Playskool and Fisher-Price catalogs. I used my own children to further my addiction.

Al: To everyone on the outside, we were the all-American family. But privately, we spent anxious days and nights figuring out ways to pay for the growing expenses related to our dysfunction.

(They recreate another scene, stage left.)

Alice: I don't like those fixtures. I want the crystal and brass ones from the *Better Homes & Garden* ad we saw.

Al: Hon, with all these changes we're making on the plans, we're going to go another $50,000 in debt on this house.

Alice: Al, I can't live there knowing what's on the market but not on our house.

Al: Alice, you are absolutely driving me . . . *(looking around)* Where's the *Sharper Image* catalog? I have to steady my nerves.

Alice: Look, why don't you get a decent job where you can make us some money?

Al: Look who's talking! Every job you get, they fire you. What was it last time— your manager catching you in the back room high from the scratch and sniff ads in *Vogue*? If you don't keep a job long enough to help pay for all this, we're going to have to dip into Jimmy's savings account just to stay afloat. Speaking of Jimmy, where is he?

Alice: How should I know? You're the one that picked him up after soccer practice.

Al: Me? You were supposed to get him on your way back from the grocery store.

Alice: I told you before I left I wouldn't have time.

Al: "Wouldn't have time"? You were gone for three and a half hours. What did you do after you—no, you didn't! You stopped at the new models going up on Hastings Road! No wonder the price of our house keeps going up. I told you —no more Parade of Homes!

Alice: You should talk . . . Mr. Handy Andy junky. *(He is shocked to be found out.)* Didn't think I saw you duck in there, did you? Thought you could sneak a few pints of flat latex, huh? Just a quick hit with the boys from a fifteen-dollar rebate on a new shop vac.

Al: *(like Jackie Gleason)* You're spying on me, Alice!

Alice: I can't take this anymore— I'm going to call my analyst.

Al: Fine! Have her do your colors all over again! Spend another thousand dollars on a new wardrobe so your clothes don't clash with your lovely autumn skin.

(They break to "confession scene" again.)

Alice: Things just kept getting worse.

Al: Our friends didn't help either. We started going to parties where . . . well, it's pretty hard to talk about it without getting sick.

Alice: Couples were openly swapping their . . . catalogs. We'd all sit and watch hours of taped TV with all the programs edited out so it was only the commercials.

Al: Nobody even tried to hide their excesses. I saw people snort four-inch lines of Coke . . . ads. I woke up one Monday morning literally on the floor of the back seat of my car. clutching a ragged copy of *Tradin' Times.*

Alice: Right about that time I could see I was in too deep also. One afternoon I came home right after the cleaning service had thrown out all the old catalogs. I was desperate for a glance at something, anything, but they'd even found my private stash in the cupboard. I went to my own daughter's room and stole her copy of *Seventeen* . . . I totally OD'd on Maybelline ads.

Al: We decided to check into the hospital together. We're in our third week of treatment . . . and we're going to make it.

Alice: It hasn't been easy going cold turkey. When you're an ad-aholic, all you think about is that next sale. But I don't want to be just another statistic.

Al: For me, I wanted to be like all the smiling people in the ads. I wanted to buy whatever they had that made them so happy.

Alice: We've spent our lives chasing the American dream. Now we realize . . . we can't afford it—even with a cashback bonus and low monthly payments.

Al: *(pause)* It wasn't a dream.

Alice: No, it wasn't a dream.

Both: It was a nightmare.

Fadeout

Keeping Tabs

Nancy is so compulsive in her need not to be obligated to anyone that she keeps tabs on everything she and her husband receive. When a bouquet of flowers arrives anonymously, she threatens to call the florist to find out who she "owes." Her husband confesses it was his idea "because he loves her"—and she can only speculate what he really wants from her. The sketch underscores the difficulty some people have in really understanding that some things—such as God's free gift of grace—are given with no strings attached.

SUGGESTED TOPICS: grace, marriage

CHARACTERS:

Nancy   a compulsive woman, very afraid of owing anyone anything

Dan   her loving but frustrated husband

PROPS: sofa, computer printout, newspaper, box of flowers

Keeping Tabs

Sharon Sherbondy

Setting: *Dan is sitting on a sofa reading a newspaper.*

Nancy: *(entering)* Oh, Dan.

Dan: Oh, what?

Nancy: Are you busy right now?

Dan: *(dropping paper)* Depends. Why?

Nancy: I thought today would be a good time to start planning your birthday party.

Dan: *(back to paper)* I'm busy.

Nancy: Dan.

Dan: Nancy, it's not for two months.

Nancy: I know. That's why we need to get started on it now.

Dan: Couldn't we just go out for a quiet dinner this year?

Nancy: Just the two of us?

Dan: Sorry. I must have lost my head for a moment.

Nancy: Oh, it's not that. It's just . . . Well, you know, we have to have a party.

Dan: Why?

Nancy: Because . . . well, take the Millers, for example.

Dan: For an example of what?

Nancy: Do you realize that we have been invited to their home six times in the last year?

Dan: So?

Nancy: So we've only had them here four times.

Dan: So?

Nancy: So we owe them.

Dan: Nancy, I really don't think they're keeping track.

Nancy: And then on top of that Linda calls me at least once a week.

Dan: What's wrong with that? I thought you liked her.

Nancy: I do, but I hardly ever call her.

Dan: Well, so?

Nancy: It makes me feel guilty. I don't like someone being so nice to me when I'm not as nice to them. And her calls just rub it in.

Dan: Nancy, don't you think you're being just a little neurotic?

Nancy: No. You know how people are. They keep tabs on things like invitations, gifts, and phone calls. And I'm telling you if we don't start catching up here, we're going to lose them.

Dan: Will you listen to yourself? You're talking as if we have to buy our friends.

Nancy: Not buy them, just stay even or get ahead. So, you see, that's why we have to have a party.

Dan: To pay back the Millers?

Nancy: Not just the Millers. The Whites, the Langstones, the Addisons.

Dan: And what do we "owe" the Addisons?

Nancy: Oh, honestly. Have you no cells in your brain? Don't you remember what they gave us for Christmas two years ago?

Dan: Silly me, but no, I don't.

Nancy: *(gets a computer printout form from an end table or on floor next to sofa)* All right, I'll show you.

Dan: What the heck is that?

Nancy: It's a computer printout showing what people have given us in the last few years.

Dan: *(looking at it)* You've got this alphabetized . . .

Nancy: And categorized. You see, in this column I have their name and a number which represents the number of times we've been invited to their house. I've also entered the gifts they gave us, along with the food they served. Now, over here in this column it lists the number of times we've had them here, our menu, and the gifts we gave them.

Dan: Nancy, this is ridiculous. I've never heard of anyone keeping an account like this.

Nancy: Well, maybe not like *this*, but people have it all in their heads, I guarantee you. Now look at this, Dan. Look at the number of blanks in our column compared to everyone else. See the Addisons here: three times . . . ribs, turkey, filet . . . napkin rings. Us: nothing. The Langstons: five times . . . roast pig, shish kebabs, steak, steak, steak . . . silver goblets! Us: burgers and a deck of cards. I am *so* embarrassed.

Dan: *(referring to her neuroses)* You should be.

Nancy: How are we going to pay all these people back?

Dan: We're not going to.

Nancy: What?

Dan: Honey, when someone has us over and gives us a gift, they do it because they want to.

Nancy: Oh, Dan, grow up! Nothing is given without expecting something in return. There are always strings attached. So, I've come up with an idea that I think should take care of our problems.

Dan: You set up an appointment to see a therapist?

Nancy: Dan, I'm serious.

Dan: So am I. *(doorbell rings)*

Nancy: I'll get it. *(she exits)*

Dan: *(picking up printout)* I don't believe this. What difference does it make? I mean, look at this . . . half this stuff we've sold at garage sales.

Nancy: *(entering)* Well, for heaven's sake, Dan, look at this. I got flowers. I wonder who they're from? Oh, here's the card. "To a terrific person." *(pause)* There's no name. There's no name?

Dan: Must be a secret admirer.

Nancy: Well, there has to be some mistake. I'll just call the florist.

Dan: Why?

Nancy: To see who sent them.

Dan: Why do you have to know?

Nancy: So I can return "the favor."

Dan: *(getting angry)* Nancy, will you get a hold of yourself? Someone sent you flowers simply because they like you, because they think you're a "terrific person." Why can't you just accept that?

Nancy: *(pause, we think he's getting through, then . . .)* I bet it was Lois. It would be just like her to do something like this.

Dan: Nancy, you're not listening to me.

Nancy: Well, I'll just call the florist.

Dan: OK, I sent them.

Nancy: Oh, you did not!

Dan: I did so.

Nancy: Why?

Dan: Because I love you.

Nancy: Don't be ridiculous!

Dan: *(growing angrier)* Nancy, I'll show you the receipt. I've got it in my wallet.

Nancy: *(taken aback)* You sent them?

Dan: Yeah. Sorry to disappoint you.

Nancy: *(pause, cocky)* All right, let's hear it. What do you want?

Dan: Nothing.

Nancy: Nothing. You never send me flowers. You must be after something.

Dan: I'm not "after" anything . . . *(tenderly)* except maybe you.

Nancy: Oh, so that's it!

Dan: I give up. I try to do something special for my wife because I love her and she doesn't trust me.

Nancy: *(looking through printout)* Williams, Williams. Here we are. Dan Williams.

Dan: You've got me in there too?

Nancy: Well, of course.

Dan: Forget it, forget it. *(grabs flowers)* I'm throwing these things out.

Nancy: Dan, don't be ridiculous.

Dan: *(totally exasperated)* Ridiculous. I'm not ridiculous. I just don't want you to feel obligated to "return the favor," to "even the score." I give you something simply because I love you.

Nancy: And I love you too, hon. I was just surprised, that's all. Now, come on, how about if you put these beautiful flowers in some water for me . . . please?

Dan: But . . .

Nancy: Please?

Dan: *(very reluctant)* Oh, all right. *(pause)* But I'm only doing it . . .

Both: "Because I love you."

Nancy: I know. *(He leaves. She waits until he's gone, then goes back to printout.)* Dan Williams. *(writing)* Flowers. June 14, 1993. Occasion: *(pause, looking out, reflective)* Because he loves me.

(Note: The way she says the last "Because he loves me" gives the impression that maybe she has understood Dan's point.)

Fadeout

One Step Up, One Step Down

In this narrated mime, an Everyman character faces ambition and the high price it exacts. To be at the top costs him family, friendships, and integrity—but he is left with wealth, a big office, and acceptance. Is this the satisfaction he thought success would bring?

SUGGESTED TOPICS: ambition, priorities, workaholism

CHARACTERS:

Everyman character

Three voices   represent voices of influence, ambition, compromise and other characters

Offstage narrator

PROPS: desk and chair, wastebasket, golf club, family portrait, Bible, trophy, camera, plaque, newspaper, briefcase, numerous papers, money, suit coat

One Step Up, One Step Down

Judson Poling

The narration is also included without the description to make it easier to read.

Setting: *Man stage right with golf club, the three "voices" standing in a line, upstage with their backs to the audience. Center stage is a chair and a desk with a trophy, Bible, and family portrait on it. Next to the desk is a wastebasket. Note: The narration should move rather quickly with care taken to make sure that it is adequately and precisely "filled" with appropriate mimed action. It is not necessary to use white-face make-up, but clear plastic masks for the voices works very effectively.*

(lights up on a man posed with his golf club)

Once upon a time there was a Man *(he begins to swing his golf club)* who had it all.

He had *friends* with whom he had a good time *(tries to cheat by moving the "ball," looks to see if anybody saw, they did),* but they were also very honest when he got out of line. *(sheepishly puts it back)* He had a family *(crosses to desk, picks up family portrait, admires it)* who loved him and whom he loved. He had *values (picks up Bible)* that helped him see right from wrong and make good choices. And he had *ambition (picks up trophy)*—the drive to do something significant with his life.

(Man puts on his suit coat, which is draped on chair.) In this Man's world, however, sometimes up was

down, sometimes more was less *(man sits and puts feet up on desk and looks affectionately at the "stuff" of his life)*, and sometimes keeping was losing. But for now he had it all, and he was happy. *(hands behind head, content)*

One day the Man heard some voices. *(Three voices face front, man swivels in his chair to face each person as he or she "speaks.")* "Come up here," they called out to him. *(Voice One gestures.)* "Climb the ladder—there's a magnificent view!" *(Voice Two gestures.)* "You're just the man who can do it, too." *(Voice Three gestures thumbs up.)* So the Man who had it all set out to go up the ladder. *(Man stands back to audience, crosses to Voice One with his golf club.)*

"If you're going to come up here where it's tough, you may have to give up some friendships. *(Voice takes man's club.)* Prospects *(gesture with club)*, contacts *(gesture)*, and business loads *(gesture)* are all the relationships you'll need." *(Flips club and taps him on chest, then waits, resting on club.)*

The Man *(steps forward and thinks)* thought this was a tough price to pay, but he reasoned, "I could use some new relationships." So the Man stopped seeing his friends *(waves good-bye, then voice leads man to "key" people, mime shaking hands, slapping on back, etc.)* and soon was spending all his time with "key people" and "important contacts." They mostly shook his hand, took him out to dinner *(man laughs at a joke)*, and made him lots of money. *(Voice One pulls out a cigar, gives it to man, mimes lighting it.)* They knew it wasn't good business to be honest with him. Soon the Man actually began to feel good about himself *(man coughs)*. But *(man crosses to chair, sits)* this was a funny world where up was sometimes down, *(Voice One begins to cross toward desk with club)*, so as the Man took his first step up the ladder, he took his first step down into the pit. *(Voice One dumps club in waste basket and walks back to his spot. This action is underscored by the haunting sound of wind blowing.)*

Soon the Man was successful and popular *(Voices One and Three cross and congratulate him)*, and the voices praised his efforts and assured him he was on his way. *(Both voices point out as though showing the man a vision.)* As he got ready to take his next move up the ladder, another voice spoke to him. *(Voice Two crosses to him, carrying a brief-*

case loaded with work, as Voice One and Three go to the side and look on.)

"If you're going to come up here where it's tough *(gesture)*, you may have to give some family time up. *(Voice picks up portrait as though saying, "This will have to go.")* Come in early *(look at watch)*, go home late, half days on Sundays. *(gestures)* Won't have much time left for family fun days." *(holds out picture)*

At first the Man thought the voice was wrong. *(Man shakes head, takes portrait back.)* He believed he could do it all. But the work kept piling up *(Voice Two opens briefcase and piles work on desk)*, and so without even realizing what he was doing *(man moves portrait over and starts digging into the stack of work)*, he eventually set aside his family. But by the time he saw his mistake, he was steeped in his own rationalizations. "They never understood me anyway," he said to himself. *(Voice Two picks up pushed-aside picture, crosses to wastebasket.)* And so in that world where more is sometimes less, the Man took another step up the ladder, and another step down into the pit. *(Again with wind sound under, the voice drops picture in basket. The man and voice lock eyes briefly.)*

(The three voices converge on the man's chair and roll him stage left.) By now the Man was well known for his great accomplishments. The voices of appreciation were even louder. *(Voice Two hands him a plaque taken from his briefcase.)* "He can do no wrong," they cried. *(Voice One snaps his picture.)* They shouted so loud, the Man had a hard time not believing his own press releases. *(Voice Three gives him a paper with his picture and story—he smiles, "I am something, aren't I?")* He decided to move up another rung on the ladder *(the three voices applaud his accomplishments)*, and again a voice spoke to him.

(Third Voice pulls him aside furtively.) "If you're going to come up here where it's tough, you may have to give up some scruples. *(Voice Three picks up Bible, shakes head, sets Bible down.)* Decisions can't always follow the book. *(Voice's hand goes to his lapel, pats it, as though he has some bribe money.)* Some jobs must get done by hook or by crook." *(He pulls out lapel, looks from side to side to see if anyone is watching.)*

The Man wanted very much to be thought of as "one of the boys." *(crosses away slightly, he thinks)* "Besides," he reasoned, "what they're asking me to do is practically legal.

(shoulder shrug, Third Voice passes him the money) The company is going to benefit *(First Voice says, "Shhh, keep this to yourself.")*, not just me." Papers were signed *(Voice Two places a paper on the desk, the man signs, handshakes all around)*, deals were made, information was withheld, and the Man *(he sits)* found that it really wasn't that hard to do after all. *(Voice Three picks up Bible and crosses to the wastebasket, as the other voices go back to their original positions.)* And so, in that world where gain is sometimes loss, the Man took another step up the ladder and moved another step down into the pit. *(With wind under, Third Voice drops Bible in trash; their eyes lock briefly.)*

As the Man looked around *(he stands)*, he realized he'd finally made it to the top. *(gesture)* He had nowhere else to go. *(Man crosses to the side, notices wastebasket filled.)* He'd given up friends, family, and morals, but he'd gotten wealth *(pats money now in his coat pocket)*, a big office, and acceptance. *(Voices now face forward and clap broadly, in slow motion. During a sustained pause, the man turns and faces each one.)* However, he was no longer the Man who had it all. *(Man is facing forward again.)* As he looked at what remained *(sees and picks up trophy)* he saw that all he had left was his ambition. No friends to correct it *(crosses toward Voice One with trophy; Voice One turns his back on him)*, no family to encourage it *(crosses toward Voice Two, who turns his back)*, no values to channel it *(crosses toward Voice Three, who turns his back)*. Only raw, unrestrained ambition. *(Man crosses back to desk, reflective.)*

The Man had gone up the ladder, but now he was the fool on the hill. *(man now sitting on front of desk)* Because up is sometimes down, more is sometimes less, and the top of a ladder can sometimes be no higher than the bottom of a pit. *(Fear and emptiness are the only things he has left. The lights fade as he sits clutching the trophy.)*

(Narration only)

Once upon a time there was a Man who had it all.

He had *friends* with whom he had a good time, but they were also very honest when he got out of line. He had a *family* who loved him and whom he loved. He had *values* that helped him see right from wrong and make good choices. And he had *ambition* — the drive to do something significant with his life.

In this Man's world, however, sometimes up was down, sometimes more was less, and sometimes keeping was losing. But for now he had it all, and he was happy.

One day the Man heard some voices. "Come up here," they called out to him. "Climb the ladder — there's a magnificent view!" "You're just the man who can do it, too." So the Man who had it all set out to go up the ladder.

"If you're going to come up here where it's tough, you may have to give some friendships up. Prospects, contacts, and business leads are all the relationships you'll need."

The Man thought this was a tough price to pay, but he reasoned, "I could use some new relationships." So the Man stopped seeing his friends and soon was spending all his time with "key" people" and "important contacts." They mostly shook his hand, took him out to dinner, and made him lots of money. They knew it wasn't good business to be honest with him. Soon the Man actually began to feel good about himself. But this was a funny world where up was sometimes down, so as the Man took his first step up the ladder, he took his first step down into the pit.

Soon the Man was successful and popular, and the voices praised his efforts and assured him he was on his way. As he got ready to take his next move up the ladder, another voice spoke to him.

"If you're going to come up here where it's tough, you may have to give some family time up. Come in early, go home late, half days on Sundays. Won't have much time left for family fun days."

At first the Man thought the voice was wrong. He believed he could do it all. But the work kept piling up, and so without even realizing what he was doing, he eventually set aside his family. But by the time he saw his mistake, he was steeped in his own rationalizations. "They never understood me anyway," he said to himself. And so in that world where more is sometimes less, the Man took another step up the ladder, and another step down into the pit.

By now the Man was well known for his great accomplishments. The voices of appreciation were even louder. "He can do no wrong," they cried. They shouted so loud, the Man had a hard time not believing his own press releases. He decided to move up another rung on the ladder, and again a voice spoke to him.

"If you're going to come up here where it's tough, you may have to give up some scruples. Decisions can't always follow the book. Some jobs must get done by hook or by crook."

The Man wanted very much to be thought of as "one of the boys." "Besides," he reasoned, "what they're asking me to do is practically legal. The company is going to benefit, not just me." Papers were signed, deals were made, information was withheld, and the Man found that it really wasn't that hard to do after all. And so, in that world where gain is sometimes loss, the Man took another step up the ladder and moved another step down into the pit.

As the Man looked around, he realized he'd finally made it to the top. He had nowhere else to go. He'd given up friends, family, and morals, but he'd gotten wealth, a big office, and acceptance. However, he was no longer the Man who had it all. As he looked at what remained, he saw that all he had left was his ambition. No friends to correct it, no family to encourage it, no values to channel it. Only raw, unrestrained ambition.

The Man had gone up the ladder, but now he was the fool on the hill. Because up is sometimes down, more is sometimes less, and the top of a ladder can sometimes be no higher than the bottom of a pit.

Driven

In the car on the way to a sales awards banquet, Doug and Nancy get in a fight. She is becoming more and more frightened of the man he's becoming as he claws his way to success. Everybody around him is paying a price for his achievements, and he can't see it. In the end, Nancy gets out of the car, unable to tolerate his success act any longer. As the lights fade, Doug lays on the horn, frustrated and alone.

SUGGESTED TOPICS: workaholism, marriage, anger

CHARACTERS:

Doug	a driven-to-achieve businessman
Nancy	a driven-to-desperation wife

PROPS: two chairs

Driven

Donna Hinkle Lagerquist

Setting: *Couple driving in a car, dressed up for a banquet. The car can simply be two chairs placed side by side. Steering wheel is mimed.*

Doug: What cross street is it on?

Nancy: *(looking at directions)* It doesn't say.

Doug: What do you mean it doesn't say?

Nancy: All it says is 2218 Main Street.

Doug: East Main Street or West Main Street?

Nancy: It doesn't say . . . all it says is 22 . . .

Doug: *(irritated, interrupting her)* Never mind, I'll find it. The least they could do is give you directions . . . numbers don't mean a thing in this city.

Nancy: Why don't we stop at that gas station and ask?

Doug: I'll find it.

Nancy: *(pause, looking out window)* Didn't we already pass by that funeral home?

Doug: No.

Nancy: That's funny. I could have sworn we did . . . I remember that big green banner

— I thought it was odd for a funeral home to have it on their door.

Doug: Nancy, I know where I'm going . . . Are you insinuating that I'm driving around in circles?

Nancy: I'm not insinuating . . .

Doug: Besides, there are hundreds of funeral homes on this street. You're wrong.

Nancy: *(pause)* I'm not arguing . . . Will you please "nicen" up a bit? I mean, we are going to an award banquet for you—that should make you happy.

Doug: *(not convincing)* I'm happy. I worked hard for this. I am very happy . . . I wish I could say the same for other members of this family.

Nancy: What?

Doug: You know what I mean . . . Here I am being honored as top salesman third year running and the people at work are more excited than my own family!

Nancy: That's not true!

Doug: Oh, yeah? Then where are Scott and Kyle?

Nancy: Doug, last year they were the only children there!

Doug: Hank Grenley's daughter was there.

Nancy: She's twenty-five years old! And besides, you know that Scott has an algebra test tomorrow and Kyle, if you remember, spilled his water three times during the dinner last year. He just gets too antsy to sit through these things.

Doug: You see, that's where they get that attitude right there . . . you talk about "these things" like they are a drudgery . . . if you didn't want to go, why didn't you say so?

(Nancy turns to respond but doesn't; there is a long pause.)

Doug: *(very impatient)* C'mon. C'mon . . . what's wrong with these lights here? They're longer than a freight train.

Nancy: *(hesitant)* Because I'm afraid of you.

Doug: What?

Nancy: Because I'm afraid of you.

Doug: What are you talking about?

Nancy: I didn't tell you I didn't want to go tonight because I was afraid to . . . just like I am afraid to tell you that we just passed by the funeral home with the green banner on the door again. I'm afraid to tell you anything you don't want to hear anymore, Doug! I'm afraid of you . . . of who you have become! *(growing anger)* Stop this car! I want to get out!

Doug: Nancy, will you calm down!

Nancy: I can't calm down, Doug . . . not anymore . . . stop this car or I'll jump out while it's moving!

(Doug pulls over and locks the door.)

Nancy: Unlock the doors!

Doug: Nancy . . . what is the matter with you?

Nancy: Unlock the doors or I'll scream!

Doug: You're already screaming! Now, will you please tell me what's going on here? I ask a simple question and you start getting hysterical! Is this some kind of change of life thing? Aren't you a little young for that?

Nancy: *(looks at him, shakes her head, tries to maintain her composure)* Yes, yes. It's a change of life thing all right . . . but not *my* life . . . yours! Doug, ten years ago if I had a headache you'd kiss my forehead to make it better and I loved it, it showed you cared.

Doug: *(sarcastic)* So, I haven't been caring enough, is that it?

Nancy: Listen to you . . . the sarcasm, the anger . . . it doesn't stop. What's happened to you? You've turned into this cold

Nancy: machine . . . driven by success . . . out to prove you don't need anyone's help . . . out to make a sale at any cost . . . out to win at any price . . . who are you trying to please? Certainly not me or the boys! Your father?

Doug: He's dead, Nancy.

Nancy: He's the one that convinced you that teaching was a dead end job—something you should take up when you fail at what you really want to do! But you really wanted to teach . . . and you were good.

Doug: (baffled) Why are you bringing this up now?

Nancy: And we were happy.

Doug: We were poor.

Nancy: We were happy.

Doug: Nancy—don't make it out to be so wonderful—you wouldn't have your car or your house if I hadn't gone to work for him . . . do you remember that? No, it wasn't a bed of roses!

Nancy: I remember a man who loved playing with his boys, a man whose eyes lit up when he talked about his students . . . We didn't have much money, but we did have *you*.

Doug: Your timing is great, Nancy . . . I'm on my way to get honored, and you're ripping me to shreds . . . can we at least get to the banquet, fake like we're happy, and talk about this later?

Nancy: This didn't just happen, Doug. It's been happening for years . . . you're still proving yourself to your father, and you're shredding yourself in the process. I can't stand to watch you anymore . . . I hate what you've become!

(Pause, he unlocks the door, calling her bluff. She goes for the door.)

Doug: *(grabs her arm)* Nancy . . .

Nancy: *(pulls her arm away)* No, I wish I could bring the old Doug back . . . but I can't. I don't believe it's even possible. Bye, Doug. *(She gets out of car, closes door, and walks off. Doug, now totally frustrated, takes a moment, looking after her, and then not knowing how else to express his anger, lays on the horn as the lights fade.)*

WILLOW CREEK RESOURCES

This resource was created to serve you.

It is just one of many ministry tools that are part of the Willow Creek Resources® line, published by the Willow Creek Association together with Zondervan Publishing House. The Willow Creek Association was created in 1992 to serve a rapidly growing number of churches from all across the denominational spectrum that are committed to helping unchurched people become fully devoted followers of Christ. There are now more than 2,500 WCA member churches worldwide.

The Willow Creek Association links like-minded leaders with each other and with strategic vision, information, and resources in order to build prevailing churches. Here are some of the ways it does that:

- **Church Leadership Conferences**—3 1/2 -day events, held at Willow Creek Community Church in South Barrington, IL, that are being used by God to help church leaders find new and innovative ways to build prevailing churches that reach unchurched people.

- **The Leadership Summit**—a once-a-year event designed to increase the leadership effectiveness of pastors, ministry staff, volunteer church leaders, and Christians in business.

- **Willow Creek Resources®**—to provide churches with a trusted channel of ministry resources in areas of leadership, evangelism, spiritual gifts, small groups, drama, contemporary music, and more. For more information, call Willow Creek Resources® at 800/876-7335. Outside the US call 610/532-1249.

- *WCA News*—a bimonthly newsletter to inform you of the latest trends, resources, and information on WCA events from around the world.

- *The Exchange*—our classified ads publication to assist churches in recruiting key staff for ministry positions.

- **The Church Associates Directory**—to keep you in touch with other WCA member churches around the world.

- *WillowNet*—an Internet service that provides access to hundreds of Willow Creek messages, drama scripts, songs, videos and multimedia suggestions. The system allows users to sort through these elements and download them for a fee.

- *Defining Moments*—a monthly audio journal for church leaders, in which Lee Strobel asks Bill Hybels and other Christian leaders probing questions to help you discover biblical principles and transferable strategies to help maximize your church's potential.

For conference and membership information please write or call:

Willow Creek Association
P.O. Box 3188
Barrington, IL 60011-3188
ph: (847) 765-0070
fax: (847) 765-5046
www.willowcreek.org

0597

Other Willow Creek Resources™ Available

An Inside Look at the Willow Creek Seeker Service Video

An Inside Look at the Willow Creek Worship Service Video

One-on-One with Oliver North Video (an interview with Bill Hybels)

Sunday Morning Live, Volume 1

Sunday Morning Live, Volume 2

Sunday Morning Live Video, Volume 1

Sunday Morning Live Video, Volume 2

Sunday Morning Live Video, Volume 3

Walking With God Journal

Walking With God Series
> *Building Your Church*
> *Discovering the Church*
> *"Follow Me!"*
> *Friendship With God*
> *Impacting Your World*
> *The Incomparable Jesus*
> *Leader's Guide 1*
> *Leader's Guide 2*

Individual Drama Sketches Available

A listing and description of the over 200 Willow Creek drama sketches is now available from Willow Creek Resources™. These sketches provide a visually powerful way to introduce and reinforce a variety of biblical topics of interest to seekers and believers alike. Each is written to correspond with a message given by the pastor.

To obtain a free copy of this catalog, or for more information, call 1-800-876-SEEK (7335).